GROWTH OF MOTORCYCLE USE IN METRO MANILA

IMPACT ON ROAD SAFETY

JULY 2020

ASIAN DEVELOPMENT BANK

Contents

Tables and Figures

Abbreviations

EDSA	–	Epifanio de los Santos Avenue
GNI	–	gross national income
JICA	–	Japan International Cooperation Agency
MMARAS	–	Metro Manila Accident Reporting and Analysis System
MMDA	–	Metropolitan Manila Development Authority
NCR	–	National Capital Region
WHO	–	World Health Organization

Introduction

This study aims to characterize the utilization of motorcycles in Metro Manila to provide better appreciation of its phenomenal growth as a form of public of transport for daily commuting. By understanding the factors that led to the increased usage of motorcycles, it is hoped that this will contribute to policy and infrastructure initiatives and address this trend in the context of behavioral strategies.

Information from the World Health Organization was used to show the comparative increase in motorcycle usage, followed by a discussion on motorcycle and road safety. With utilization of motorcycles or two-wheeled vehicles in Metro Manila being the main focus, the study discusses (i) the behavior of persons using motorcycles or two-wheeled vehicles, either for mobility or commercial purposes, and (ii) trends or developments in the use of two-wheeled vehicles as a mode of transport.

Global Motorcycle Usage

Asia, as a whole, has the most number of registered motorcycles as shown by the total registered vehicles in 2013 and in 2016 (Table 1). The worldwide population increased by 4.10% from 2013 to 2016, and roughly the same for Asia (3.89%) and Southeast Asia (3.72%) (Table 2). During this 3-year period, the total registered vehicles increased by 12.44% worldwide, and by 18.78% in Asia and by 22.16% in Southeast Asia.

The number of registered motorcycles also increased significantly worldwide by 24.74% from 2013 to 2016. In particular, the increase in registered motorcycles is higher than the increase in total registered vehicles for Asia, Central America, Europe, Oceania, and South America. In the Philippines, the increase in registered motorcycles is likewise higher than the increase in total registered vehicles, indicating that Filipinos are opting to use motorcycles for mobility.

Table 1: Total Registered Vehicles and Registered Motorcycles, 2013 and 2016

Continent/ Area	2013			2016		
	Population	Vehicles	Motorcycles	Population	Vehicles	Motorcycles
Asia	4,231,620,460	862,391,534	321,945,349	4,396,231,185	1,024,309,230	407,677,238
Middle East	42,671,027	12,275,280	289,182	48,761,765	14,970,962	354,483
Southeast Asia	618,374,908	218,233,129	166,499,218	641,352,601	266,601,274	201,688,136
Philippines	98,393,547	7,690,038	4,250,667	103,320,224	9,521,565	5,329,770
Africa	818,574,154	36,246,073	9,160,662	898,411,546	50,662,954	11,351,846
Central America	186,057,263	47,032,333	5,278,220	194,115,520	54,691,754	7,050,120
North America	355,232,420	287,409,632	9,098,954	358,469,440	305,236,252	9,310,194
South America	376,082,211	129,352,842	36,457,924	388,611,245	147,638,761	45,727,052
Europe	544,541,540	339,141,924	32,713,428	543,077,921	356,984,397	39,029,910
Oceania	35,691,800	20,574,804	868,741	37,410,630	22,138,750	967,456
World	**6,547,799,848**	**1,744,592,976**	**417,754,454**	**6,816,327,487**	**1,961,662,098**	**521,113,816**

Note: Computed data on the number of vehicles and motorcycles for both 2013 and 2016 include only countries with said data in their respective country profiles, as presented in the 2015 and 2018 World Health Organization (WHO) Global Status Report on Road Safety. Figures from said reports account for total registered vehicles only. It was also mentioned that the most recent available data at the time of publication were used. In completing the above table, the number of motorcycles for countries without breakdown of vehicles by type was estimated based on the same growth rate as the vehicles. Motorcycles in the table above are labeled as two- and three-wheelers in the WHO reports.

Source: World Health Organization. *Global Status Report on Road Safety*. Geneva (2015 and 2018).

Table 2: Percentage Change of Total Registered Vehicles and Registered Motorcycles, 2013–2016
(%)

Continent/Area	Population	Vehicles	Motorcycles
Asia	3.89	18.78	26.63
Middle East	14.27	21.96	22.58
Southeast Asia	3.72	22.16	21.13
Philippines	5.01	23.82	25.39
Africa	9.75	39.78	23.92
Central America	4.33	16.29	33.57
North America	0.91	6.20	2.32
South America	3.33	14.14	25.42
Europe	-0.27	5.26	19.31
Oceania	4.82	7.60	11.36
World	**4.10**	**12.44**	**24.74**

Source: World Health Organization. *Global Status Report on Road Safety.* Geneva (2015 and 2018).

Figure 1 illustrates the comparison between the increase in registered motorcycles and increase in total registered vehicles. Compared to total registered vehicles, the percentage increase in registered motorcycles is higher in Asia, Central America, South America, Europe, and Oceania, and lower in Africa and North America. Although the percentage increase in total registered vehicles is slightly higher in Southeast Asia, the Philippines, which is part of the region, has shown a higher percentage increase in registered motorcycles than the total registered vehicles. This supports the assumption that preference for motorcycles in the Philippines is becoming significant. The study shows that motorcycles have become essential in the daily activities of a growing number of Filipinos, which can be attributed to the lack of better and effective public transport systems.

Figure 1: Percentage Change of Total Registered Vehicles and Registered Motorcycles, 2013 and 2016

(%)

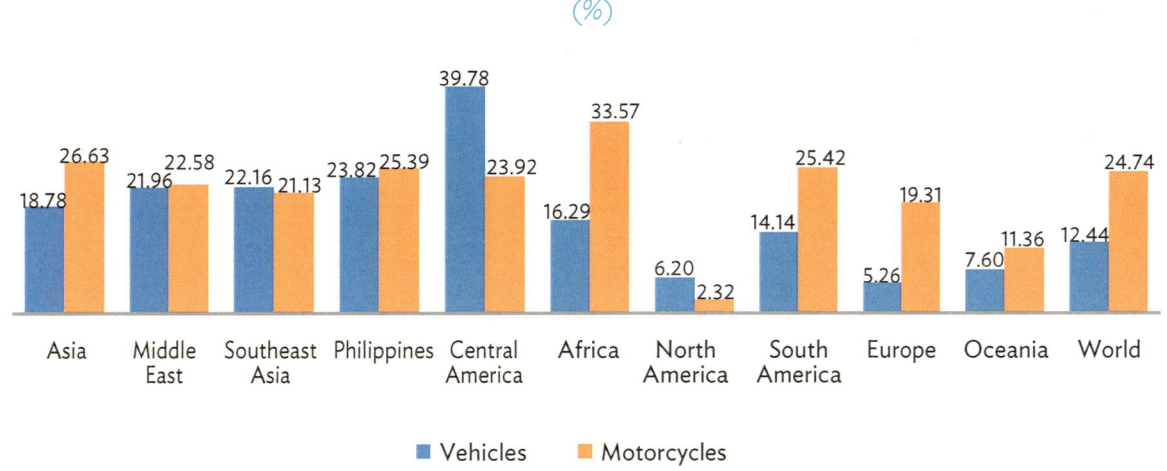

Source: World Health Organization. *Global Status Report on Road Safety.* Geneva (2015 and 2018).

Calculating the number of vehicles per 1,000 population (Figure 2) points to the following observations:

- There were fewer than 300 vehicles for every 1,000 population in the world in 2016, or a ratio of about 1 vehicle for every 4 persons. The vehicle to population ratio from 2013 to 2016 is almost the same worldwide.

- The motorcycle to population ratio worldwide in 2016 was 1 motorcycle for every 13 persons, a significant decrease from the motorcycle to population ratio of 1:16 in 2013.

- Except for North America, all geographic areas show a similar trend of an increase in the number of motorcycles per 1,000 population. This shows that motorcycle use is becoming a major option in the mobility of people, particularly in the growing economies of Asia, Africa, and South America.

Figure 2: Vehicles and Motorcycles per 1,000 Population by Region, 2013 and 2016

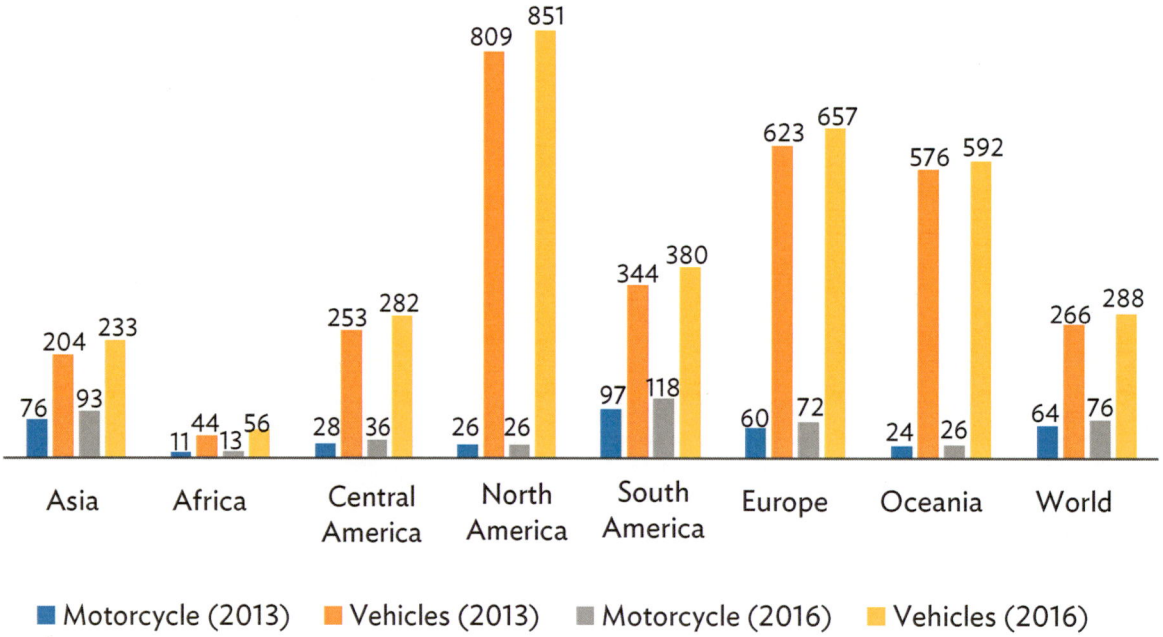

Source: Asian Development Bank, as adapted from the 2015 and 2018 editions of the *Global Status Report on Road Safety* by the World Health Organization.

The top 20 countries with the highest number of motorcycles per 1,000 population in 2016 are shown in Figure 3, with Viet Nam having the highest at 498. Six out of the 20 countries are in Southeast Asia (Viet Nam, Indonesia, Malaysia, Thailand, Lao People's Democratic Republic, and Cambodia), which indicates significant motorcycle usage in the region. Figure 3 shows that Viet Nam had the highest number of motorcycles per 1,000 population in 2016, with 90 vehicles higher than the second-ranked Indonesia.

Figure 3: Top 20 Countries with Highest Number of Motorcycles per 1,000 Population, 2016

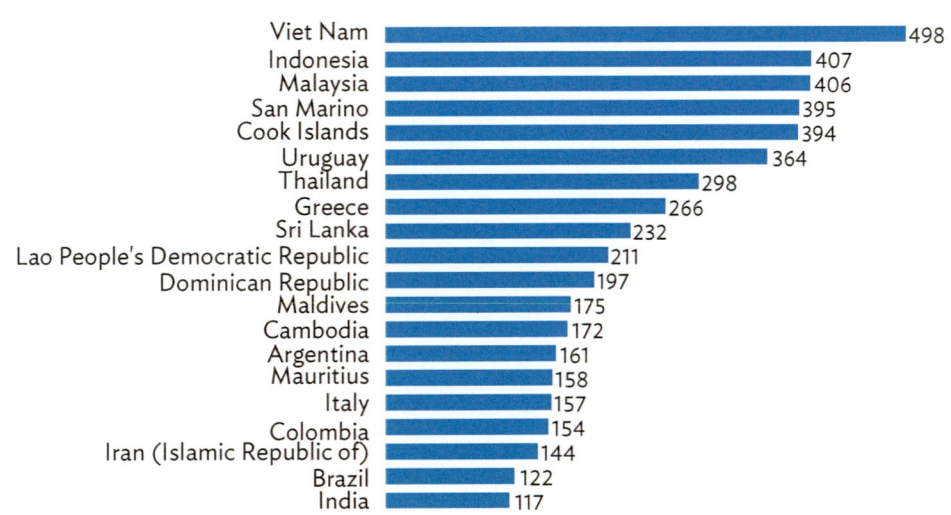

Source: World Health Organization. *Global Status Report on Road Safety.* Geneva (2015 and 2018).

Focusing on Southeast Asia, Table 3 and Figure 4 show that:

- Malaysia had the highest number vehicles per 1,000 population in 2013 and 2016. It also ranks third among countries worldwide with the highest number of motorcycles per 1,000 population.

- Viet Nam had the highest number of motorcycles per 1,000 population in the world. With motorcycles almost equal to vehicles per 1,000 population, this indicates that the motorcycle is among the most utilized vehicles in the country.

- The Philippines was among the countries with the lowest number of vehicles and motorcycles per 1,000 population. Nevertheless, it is worth noting that the number of motorcycles per 1,000 population was about half of the vehicles per 1,000 population in the Philippines.

- Singapore has fewer motorcycles per 1,000 population compared to the other countries.

Table 3: Number of Motorcycles in Relation to Gross National Income per Capita, ASEAN

Country/Area	Motorized Two- to Three-Wheelers per 1,000 Population	GNI per Capita ($)	Income Level[a]
Cambodia	172	1,140	Middle
Indonesia	407	3,400	Middle
Lao People's Democratic Republic	211	2,150	Middle
Malaysia	406	9,850	Middle
Myanmar	102	1,190	Middle
Philippines	52	3,580	Middle
Singapore	25	51,880	High
Thailand	298	5,640	Middle
Timor-Leste	85	2,180	Middle
Viet Nam	498	2,050	Middle

ASEAN = Association of Southeast Asian Nations, GNI = gross national income.

[a] Income classification used based on World Development Indicators database where low income means GNI equal to $1,005 or less, middle income is $1,006 to $12,235, and high income is $12,236 and above.

Source: World Health Organization. *Global Status Report on Road Safety.* Geneva (2015 and 2018).

Figure 4: Vehicles and Motorcycles per 1,000 Population in Southeast Asia, 2013 and 2016

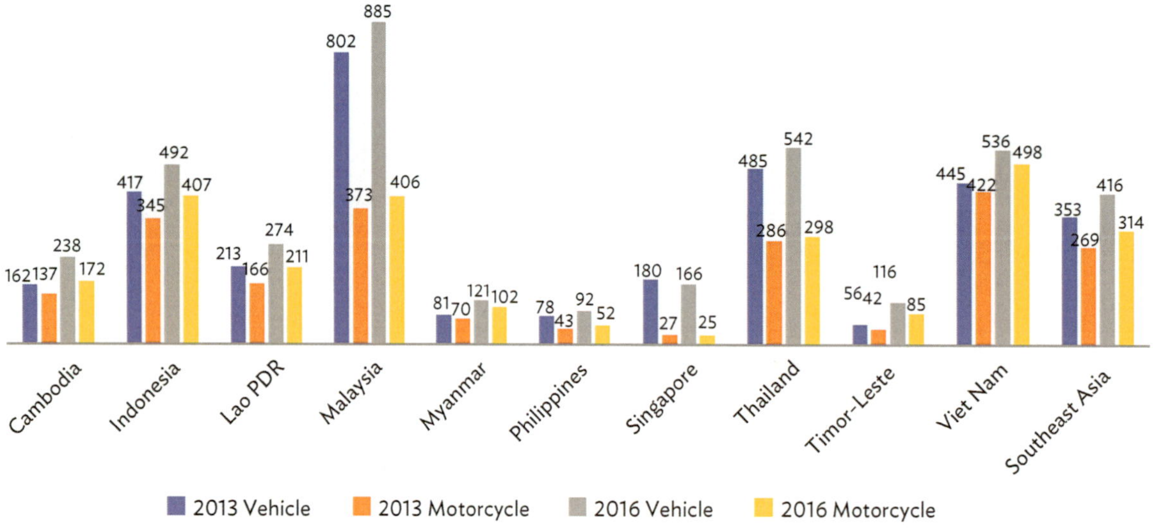

Source: World Health Organization. *Global Status Report on Road Safety.* Geneva (2015 and 2018).

Figure 5 shows that motorcycle usage is predominant in countries with lower gross national income (GNI) per capita, most of which are in Asia, Africa, and South America.

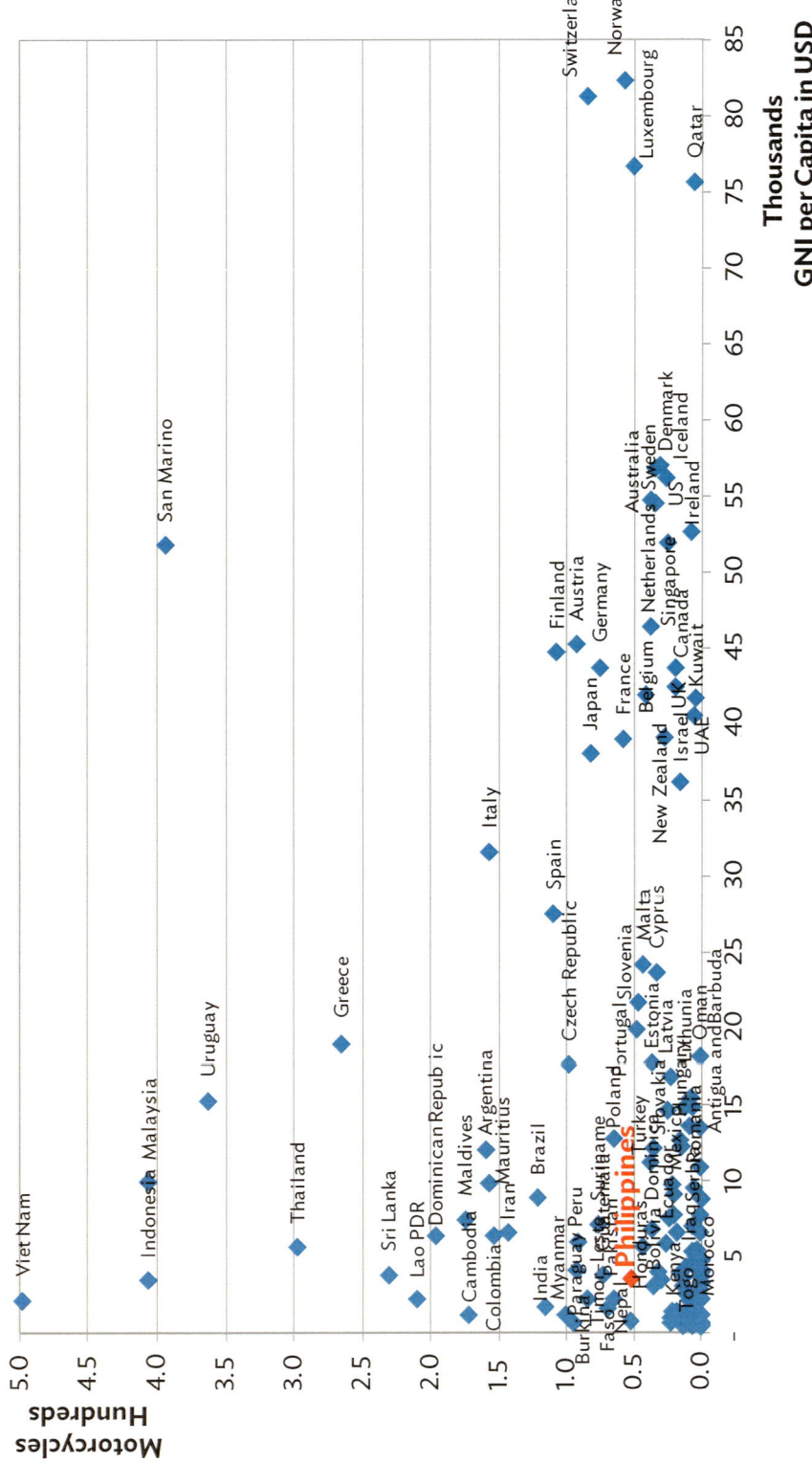

Figure 5: Motorcycles per 1,000 Population and Gross National Income per Capita, 2016

Lao PDR = Lao People's Democratic Republic, UAE = United Arab Emirates, UK = United Kingdom, US = United States.
Source: World Health Organization. *Global Status Report on Road Safety*. Geneva (2015 and 2018).

Recent Developments in Motorcycle Usage in Metro Manila

In the Philippines Census conducted in 2010, households were asked what convenience devices they own (Table 4). Respondents to the census considered the motorcycle a convenience device. Census findings are as follows:

- Almost 90% of households in the Philippines—more than 13% of which are based in Metro Manila—own at least one household convenience device.

- The five regions in the Philippines with the most number of households and, correspondingly, the most number of households that own convenience devices, are the National Capital Region (NCR) or Metro Manila, Southern Tagalog, Central Luzon, Western Visayas, and Central Visayas.

- In the Philippines, about 10% (around 1.74 million) of households indicated that they own cars while close to 22% (around 3.96 million) reported that they own motorcycles. The same observation that more households have motorcycles than cars also applies to the other regions outside of the top five.

- Roughly 14% (377,224) of households in Metro Manila reported that they own cars, exceeding the country percentage, while almost 12% (316,893) own motorcycles.

- Some regions outside Metro Manila showed significantly higher numbers of households with motorcycles than NCR.

The observations noted from Table 5 suggested that even in 2010, motorcycles had started to be an important component of a household in the Philippines. In many provinces, people have resorted to using motorcycles for mobility in the absence of an efficient public transport system. These are in the forms of tricycles, *habal-habal*, and *motorelas*,[1] among others. Recently, *bajaj* (coined from a motorcycle brand manufactured in India) has had presence in the Philippines, notably in the provinces.

In addition, the increase in usage of motorcycles in highly urban areas and metropolitan regions can also be attributed to other factors such as the use of motorcycles as delivery mode for internet or online purchases. These are points of discussions from hereon, with Metro Manila as the case study.

---

[1] *Habal-habal* refers to two-wheeled motorcycles used as public transport wherein passengers ride at the back of the driver. *Motorelas* are high-occupancy tricycles while *bajaj* refers to three-wheeled vehicles imported from India.

Table 4: Number of Households with Convenience Devices, 2010

Region	Total Number of Households	Households with At Least One Household Convenience Device	Presence of Household Conveniences/Devices														Households without Any Household Convenience Device
			Radio/Radio Cassette	Television Set	CD/DVD/VCD Player	Component/Stereo Set	Landline/Wireless Telephone	Cellular Phone	Personal Computer	Refrigerator/Freezer	Cooking Range	Washing Machine	Car/Jeep/Van	Motorcycle/Tricycle	Motorized Boat/Banca	
Philippines	20,171,899	18,143,364	12,955,187	14,624,406	10,901,385	4,674,290	1,759,677	14,668,545	2,739,022	7,776,266	5,322,354	6,072,206	1,744,329	3,955,205	618,918	2,028,535
NCR	2,759,829	2,706,439	1,966,131	2,572,597	2,017,459	964,218	700,977	2,460,979	763,366	1,587,720	1,202,149	1,501,050	377,224	316,893	25,053	53,390
CAR	352,403	320,519	261,158	231,444	193,271	60,973	15,883	270,504	53,458	130,503	147,476	109,941	38,942	35,379	1,264	31,884
I - Ilocos Region	1,050,605	987,547	790,435	862,051	574,334	236,983	61,865	813,842	127,303	455,420	300,730	308,693	94,926	313,393	20,761	63,058
II - Cagayan Valley	727,327	664,678	500,779	520,548	416,877	132,694	16,789	507,569	63,391	219,782	137,532	181,923	54,249	186,470	10,150	62,649
III - Central Luzon	2,239,011	2,146,983	1,549,497	1,988,473	1,449,792	562,930	151,197	1,840,437	365,671	1,010,719	855,996	1,147,044	266,650	661,230	36,200	92,028
IV-A CALABARZON	2,833,595	2,708,384	1,900,356	2,462,255	1,827,872	818,025	343,904	2,351,833	548,969	1,449,552	1,121,787	1,287,721	344,962	527,229	62,668	125,211
IV-B MIMAROPA	602,131	501,894	298,380	307,691	247,989	83,696	11,379	378,118	38,458	130,349	75,436	117,321	23,912	132,569	57,274	100,237
V - Bicol Region	1,111,753	935,224	672,738	656,547	466,962	167,860	31,287	688,134	79,900	262,526	146,256	153,780	42,810	189,279	57,950	176,529
VI - Western Visayas	1,526,587	1,356,058	1,019,853	1,005,423	744,302	345,429	91,753	1,043,224	137,170	489,081	260,479	233,616	100,871	259,180	46,445	170,529
VII - Central Visayas	1,487,710	1,296,572	957,156	955,018	729,701	379,474	139,174	995,005	174,618	470,556	292,291	200,503	113,417	313,386	50,327	191,138
VIII - Eastern Visayas	865,657	667,960	381,418	468,326	370,362	158,779	35,769	489,837	54,895	210,945	135,795	110,048	32,991	146,720	53,518	197,697
IX - Zamboanga Peninsula	726,272	573,223	398,608	348,951	260,070	108,146	21,156	414,679	48,756	193,774	82,305	89,639	34,703	143,256	38,413	153,049
X - Northern Mindanao	917,840	778,517	529,129	570,921	424,127	196,449	46,256	591,232	87,105	318,025	141,991	174,393	62,816	165,837	17,929	139,323
XI - Davao Region	1,011,943	880,778	617,409	628,892	456,447	213,484	50,879	667,479	95,645	373,902	193,090	195,652	67,251	216,758	22,522	131,165
XII - SOCCSKSARGEN	916,038	758,783	537,072	504,292	325,637	119,943	20,952	563,526	54,502	255,608	120,137	144,637	43,559	194,141	18,222	157,255
XIII - Caraga	504,257	401,824	220,064	279,041	207,186	88,817	16,129	308,735	33,622	146,997	67,399	77,810	20,241	86,818	23,950	102,433
ARMM	538,941	457,980	355,002	261,935	188,997	36,388	4,327	283,412	12,192	70,808	41,505	38,437	24,804	66,668	76,272	80,961

ARMM = Autonomous Region of Muslim Mindanao; CALABARZON = Cavite, Laguna, Batangas, Rizal, and Quezon; CAR = Cordillera Autonomous Region; MIMAROPA = Mindoro, Marinduque, Romblon, and Palawan; NCR = National Capital Region; SOCCSKSARGEN = South Cotabato; Cotabato, Sultan Kudarat; Sarangani, and General Santos City.

Source: Government of the Philippines, Philippine Statistics Authority. 2018. *2018 Philippine Statistical Yearbook.* Quezon City.

Metro Manila or NCR is the country's center of economic activities and the location of the bulk of urban population. The profile of Metro Manila is shown in Table 5. Though NCR accounts for only 0.2% or 620 square kilometers of the total area of the Philippines, its population of almost 13 million is about 13% of the total population in the country. Metro Manila also accounts for 41.5% of the country's gross domestic product, with more than 80% generated by tertiary industries.

Table 5: Profile of Metro Manila

Area	Square kilometers	620
	% of Philippines total	0.20
Population	'000	12,877
	% of Philippines total	13
	Average growth rate[a]	1.67
Gross regional domestic product Constant prices (2000)	₱ billion	3,312
	% of Philippines total	36
	Primary[b]	0.2
	Secondary[b]	17.6
	Tertiary[b]	82.9

[a] 2010–2015, % per year.
[b] Share by sector.
Source: Government of the Philippines, Philippine Statistics Authority. 2018.

Figures 6 and 7, which are based on a study done by the Japan International Cooperation Agency (JICA) in Metro Manila and its environment, validate the relationship between population growth and density in the NCR. The growing population has led to an outward expansion, especially toward the south and the east. This expansion requires coordinated land use and transport planning to ensure that the transport system supports expansion and economic growth.

Figure 8 illustrates the trend in Metro Manila's expansion, which presents a challenge to transport planners and traffic control authorities.

Figure 6: Population Density, 2015

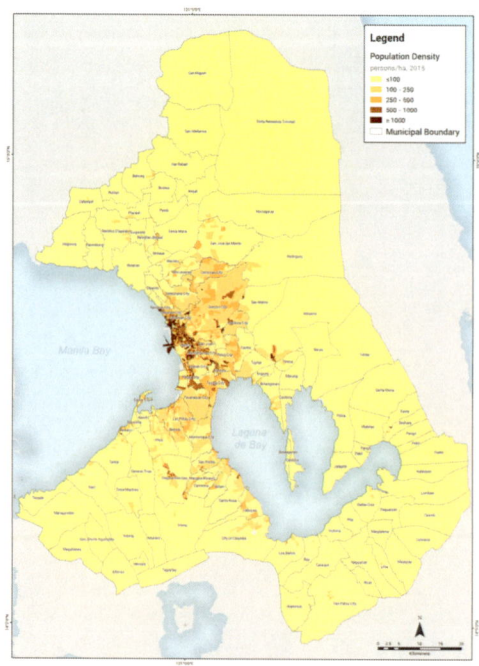

Source: Japan International Cooperation Agency. Philippines: Follow-up Survey on Roadmap for Transport Infrastructure Development for Greater Capital Region. Unpublished.

Figure 7: Population Growth, 2010–2015

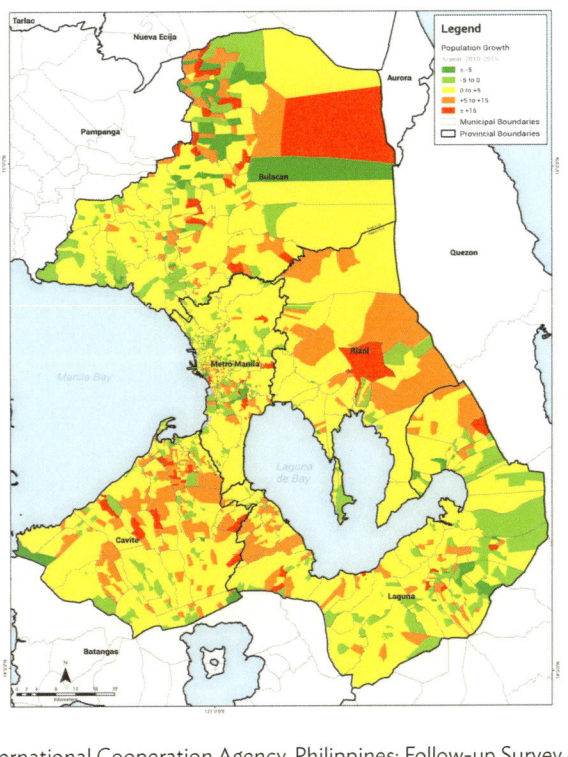

Source: Japan International Cooperation Agency. Philippines: Follow-up Survey on Roadmap for Transport Infrastructure Development for Greater Capital Region. Unpublished.

Figure 8: Urban Expansion in Metro Manila

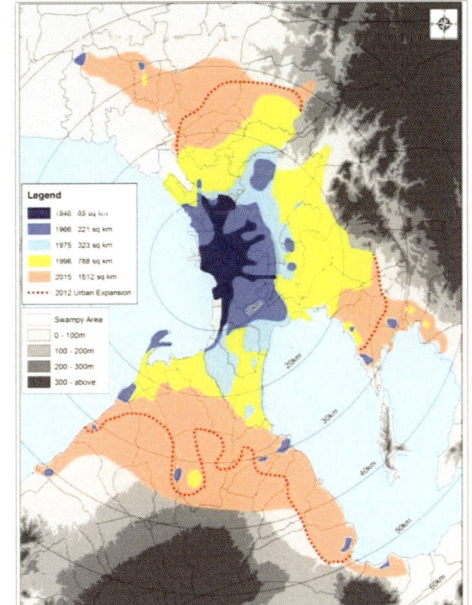

Source: Japan International Cooperation Agency. Philippines: Follow-up Survey on Roadmap for Transport Infrastructure Development for Greater Capital Region. Unpublished.

Figure 9 shows a comparison of transport modes between Metro Manila and neighboring regions. At a glance, the figure shows that the number of cars has not increased significantly, although the number of sports utility vehicles or utility vehicles has increased in Metro Manila. Meanwhile, motorcycles (including tricycles) had shown increasing overall growth, most notably in Metro Manila.

Figure 9: Number of Registered Vehicles in Metro Manila and Adjacent Regions, 2006, 2010, and 2015

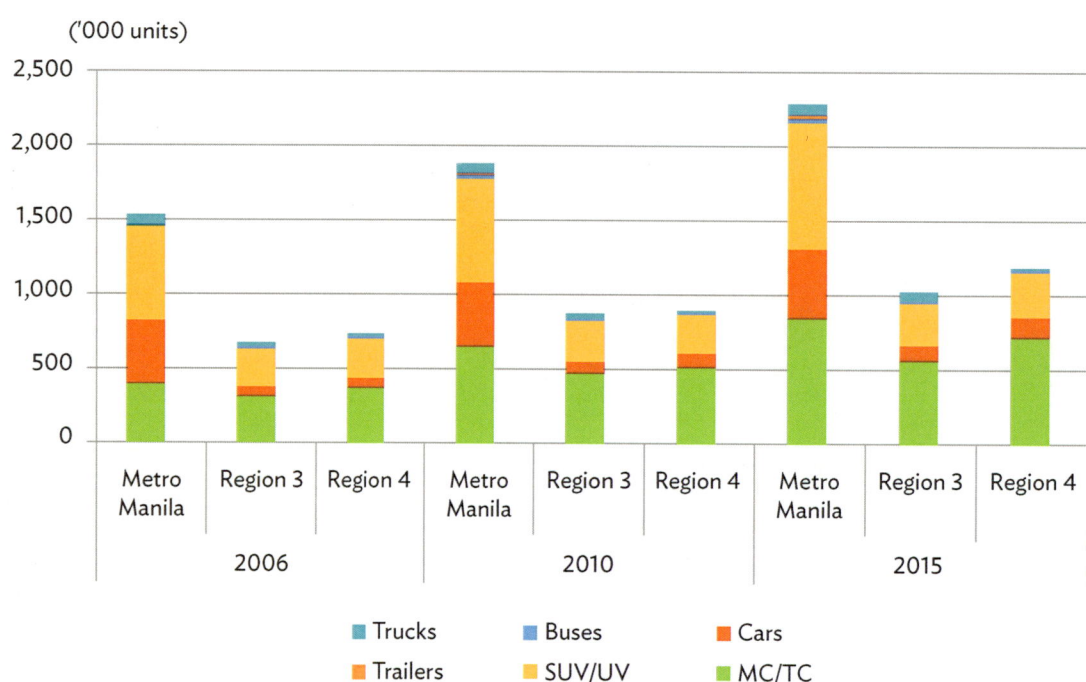

MC/TC = motorcycle/tricycle, SUV/UV = sports utility vehicle/utility vehicle.
Source: Japan International Cooperation Agency. Philippines: Follow-up Survey on Roadmap for Transport Infrastructure Development for Greater Capital Region. Unpublished. Quoted in Government of the Philippines, Philippine Statistics Authority. 2018. *2018 Philippine Statistical Yearbook*. Quezon City.

The concentration of traffic congestion in Metro Manila is in the major thoroughfares—which are also the main access leading to the ports and airport—and are part of Metro Manila's intermodal logistics network system (Figure 10). Figure 11 further elaborates the bottlenecks by showing the traffic volume and the volume–capacity ratio of the major thoroughfares in Metro Manila and Mega Manila (Metro Manila and its environs). The bottlenecks affect the economic activities and daily travel behavior of inhabitants. As mentioned, this is one of the principal reasons for the shift to motorcycles for daily commuting.

Figure 10: Bottlenecks in Metro Manila

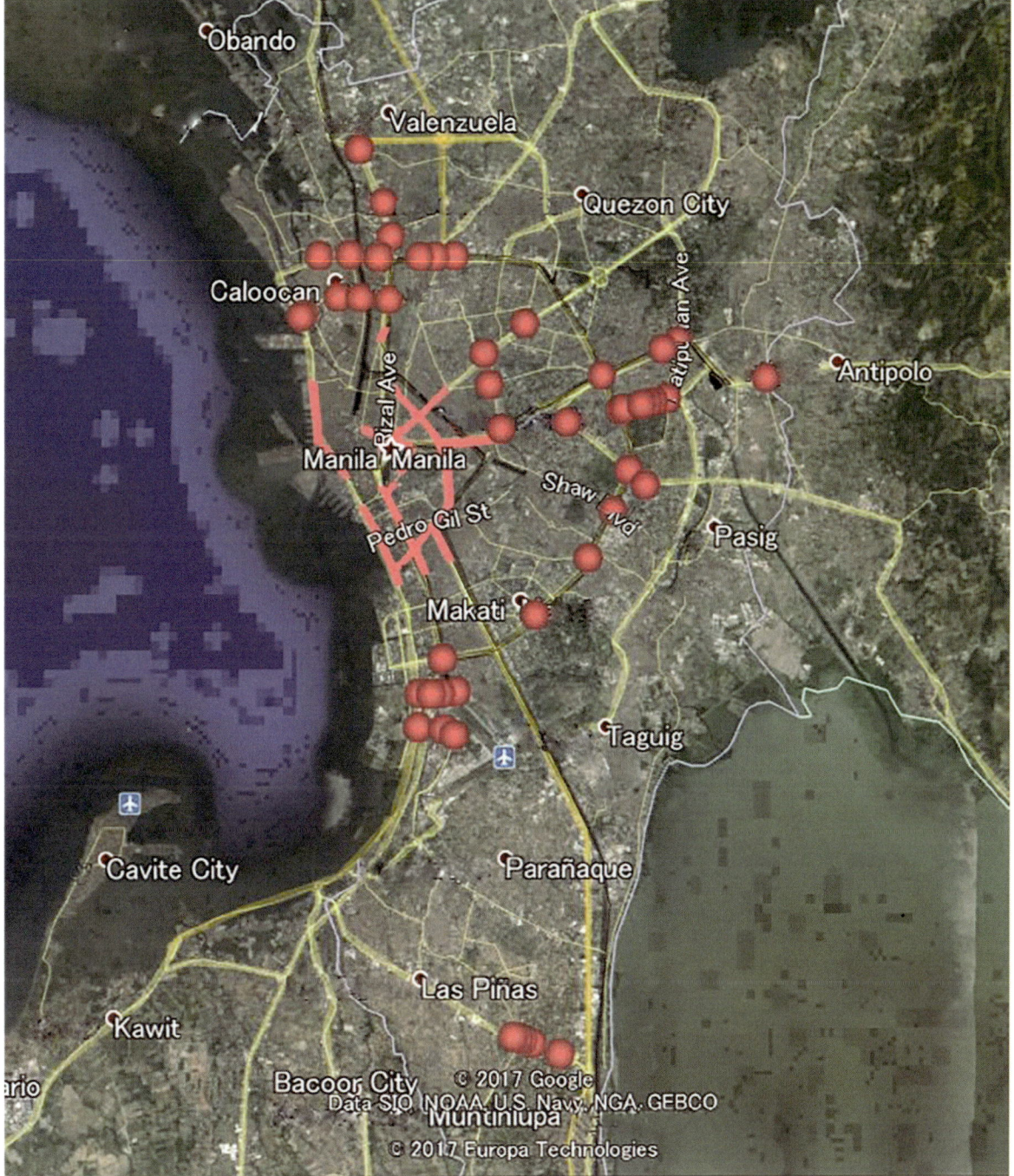

Source: Japan International Cooperation Agency. Philippines: Follow-up Survey on Roadmap for Transport Infrastructure Development for Greater Capital Region. Unpublished.

Figure 11: Traffic Volume and Volume/Capacity Ratio on Existing Road Network—Based on Traffic Model

Metro Manila   **Mega Manila**

Source: Japan International Cooperation Agency. Philippines: Follow-up Survey on Roadmap for Transport Infrastructure Development for Greater Capital Region. Unpublished.

Table 6 shows the indicators on transport impacts and denotes the economic and environmental implications of traffic congestion in Metro Manila.

Table 6: Metro Manila Comparison of Broad Indicators on Transport Outcomes, 2012, 2014, and 2017

Indicators		2012 Value	2012 Share (%)	2014 Value	2014 Share (%)	2017 Value	2017 Share (%)	14/12	17/14	17/12
Traffic Demand	Million trips per day	12.8	68.1	10.8	72.5	13.4	72.8	0.84	1.24	1.05
	Million person-km	132.0	57.7	110.0	53.6	98.5	63.0	0.83	0.90	0.75
	Million person-hour	15.0	71.4	7.7	60.6	23.0	61.0	0.51	2.99	1.53
	Million PCU-km	39.3	58.7	27.8	45.6	32.6	63.3	0.71	1.17	0.83
	Million PCU-hours	4.9	73.1	2	55.6	7.5	60.5	0.41	3.75	1.53
Volume Capacity Ratio		1.3	-	1.2	-	1.0	-	0.94	0.84	0.78
Average Travel Speed (kph)		8.0	-	14.1	-	11.9	-	1.77	0.84	1.50
Economic Cost of Transport (₱ billion per day)		2.4	70.6	1.1	52.4	3.5	60.3	0.46	3.18	1.46
Congestion Cost (₱ billion per day)		1.5	83.6	-	-	2.1	70.0	-	-	1.43
Air Quality	CO_2 (tons/day)	16,681	70.1	7,312	48.6	16,269	58.8	0.44	2.22	0.98
	NOx (tons/day)	66.0	68.0	60.0	49.4	74.3	55.7	0.90	1.25	1.13
	PM (tons/day)	2.9	70.3	2.6	52.0	3.4	54.3	0.90	1.30	1.17

CO_2 = carbon dioxide, km = kilometer, kph = kilometer per hour, NOx = nitrogen oxide, PCU = passenger car unit, PM = particulate matter.

Source: Japan International Cooperation Agency. Philippines: Follow-up Survey on Roadmap for Transport Infrastructure Development for Greater Capital Region. Unpublished.

The inclusion of two- and three-wheeled vehicles in several JICA studies relating to travel demand analyses, as reflected in Table 7, indicate that these vehicles are recognized as among the main modes of transport in Metro Manila.

Table 7: Categorization of Vehicle Types in Demand Forecast

Vehicle Types	Category in Demand Forecast		
	Roadmap 2 (2017)	MUCEP (2014)	Roadmap 1 (2013)
Motorcycle	Private	Private	Not included
Private car	Private	Private	Private
Taxi	Private	Private	Private
Jeepney	Public	Public	Public
Bus	Public	Public	Public
Truck	Private	Private	Private
Tricycle	Private	Not included	Not included

MUCEP = Metro Manila Urban Transportation Integration Study Update and Capacity Enhancement Project.
Source: Japan International Cooperation Agency. Philippines: Follow-up Survey on Roadmap for Transport Infrastructure Development for Greater Capital Region. Unpublished.

Table 8 shows travel demand in the Greater Capital Region, the expanded Metro Manila that includes nearby provinces, while Table 9 provides a summary of the results of the screen line surveys and the adjustments to provide information on the trips in Metro Manila, further supporting the notion that motorcycles are among the main modes of transport in the area.

Table 8: Travel Demand in Greater Capital Region, 2017

		2012				2017				2017/2012	
		Person Trips		PCU		Person Trips		PCU			
		No. ('000/day)	%	No. ('000/day)	%	No. ('000/day)	%	No. ('000/day)	%	Person Trips	PCU
Car		6,170	31.7	3,629	72.3	6,054	38.8	3,784	73.8	0.98	1.04
Public Transport	Jeepney	7,620	39.1	1,141	19.7	6,652	42.7	1,134	22.1	0.87	0.99
	Bus	5,680	29.2	322	8.0	2,888	18.5	211	4.1	0.51	0.66
	Subtotal	13,300	68.3	1,463	27.7	9,540	61.2	1,345	26.2	0.72	0.92
Total		19,470	100.0	5,092	100.0	15,594	100.0	5,129	100.0	0.80	1.01

PCU = passenger car unit.
Note: Data cover Metro Manila and its surrounding provinces.
Source: Japan International Cooperation Agency. Philippines: Follow-up Survey on Roadmap for Transport Infrastructure Development for Greater Capital Region. Unpublished.

Table 9: Trips Crossing Pasig River Screen Line and Adjustment Factor

Mode	Scree Line Survey Counted by Direction (trips/day)			Trips by Nonresidents (trips/day)	Trips by Residents (trips/day)	Adjustments to be 2014 (d) (trips/day)	Person Trips from HIS (trips/day)	Preliminary Adj. Factor	Applied Screen Line Adj. Factor
	N → S	S → N	Total (a)	(b)	(c=a-b)	1.035	(e)	(f=d/e)	
Pedicab	178	147	325	0	325	336	22,012	0.015	1.000
Bicycle	9,994	10,651	20,645	11	20,634	21,346	60,321	0.354	1.000
MC	100,817	100,130	200,947	1,179	199,768	206,660	478,742	0.432	1.000
Filcab+ Tricycle	14,940	16,771	31,711	239	31,472	32,558	475,937	0.068	1.000
Jeepney	205,377	227,185	432,562	1,803	430,759	445,620	1,422,218	0.313	1.000
Mini-Bus+Bus	297,146	312,152	609,298	56,653	553,098	572,180	347,487	1.647	1.647
Taxi	47,042	42,498	89,540	939	88,601	91,658	64,646	1.418	1.418
UV-HOV	39,870	46,603	86,473	251	86,222	89,197	62,430	1.429	1.429
Car	294,774	284,068	578,842	12,623	566,219	585,754	444,696	1.317	1.317
Van/ Pickup	14,434	12,681	27,115	1,937	25,178	26,047	20,919	1.245	1.245
Truck	21,165	21,934	43,099	3,514	39,585	40,951	16,704	2.452	2.452
Other	0	0	0	6,981	-6,981	-7,222	22,201	-0.325	1.000
PNR	22,171	22,171	44,342	1,534	42,808	44,285	25,734	1.721	1.721
LRT/MRT	366,231	331,398	697,629	0	697,629	721,697	268,875	2.684	2.684

HIS = household interview survey, LRT/MRT = Light Rail Transit/Metro Rail Transit, MC = motorcycle, N = north, PNR = Philippine National Railways, S = south, UV-HOV = utility vehicle-high-occupancy vehicle.

Source: Japan International Cooperation Agency. 2015. *Metro Manila Urban Transportation Integration Study Update and Capacity Enhancement Project Study*. Makati.

Looking at the number of trips by transport mode, Table 10 likewise indicates that motorcycles and cars are significant modes of private transport, while the tricycle is a significant mode of public transport, which may explain their presence in even in major thoroughfares. Table 11 further validates data in Table 10 and the previously mentioned observations.

Table 10: Trip Composition by Mode

Mode	Number of Trip ('000)	% of Public or Private	% of Total
Public Mode	17,337	100.0	48.8
Train	1,485	8.6	4.2
Bus	2,352	13.6	6.6
Jeepney	6,763	39.0	19.1
Tricycle	5,687	32.8	16.0
UV-HOV	261	1.5	0.7
Pedicab	631	3.6	1.8
Others	153	0.9	0.4
Private Mode	7,263	100.0	20.4
Motorcycle	2,948	40.6	8.3
Car	2,894	39.9	8.2
Taxi	315	4.3	0.9
Truck	270	3.7	0.8
Others	826	11.4	2.3
Walking	10,913	–	30.7
Total	**35,503**	**-**	**100.0**

UV-HOV = utility vehicle-high-occupancy vehicle.

Source: Japan International Cooperation Agency. 2015. *Metro Manila Urban Transportation Integration Study Update and Capacity Enhancement Project Study*. Makati.

Table 11: Number of Trips by Mode and Car Ownership

Mode	Non-Car Owner Number ('000)	Non-Car Owner %	Car Owner Number ('000)	Car Owner %	Total Number ('000)	Total %
Public Mode	14,667	48.2	1,603	31.7	16,270	45.9
Train	1,290	4.2	193	3.8	1,483	4.2
Bus	2,011	6.6	337	6.7	2,348	6.6
Jeepney	6,140	20.2	614	12.1	6,754	19.0
Tricycle	5,226	17.2	458	9.1	5,684	16.0
Private Mode	5,541	18.2	2,748	54.3	8,288	23.4
Car	716	2.4	2,174	43.0	2,891	8.2
Taxi	254	0.8	60	1.2	314	0.9
Truck	239	0.8	31	0.6	270	0.8
Others	4,332	14.2	482	9.5	4,814	13.6
Walking	10,201	33.5	709	14.0	10,910	30.8
Total	**30,408**	**100.0**	**5,060**	**100.0**	**35,468**	**100.0**

Source: Japan International Cooperation Agency. 2015. *Metro Manila Urban Transportation Integration Study Update and Capacity Enhancement Project Study*. Makati.

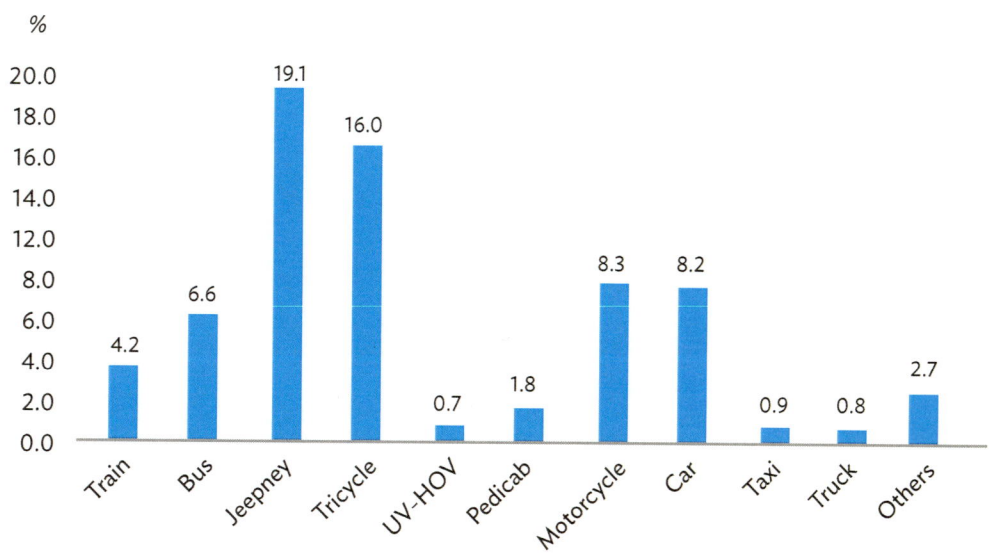

Figure 12: Shares of Public and Private Transport by Mode

UV-HOV = utility vehicle–high-occupancy vehicle.
Source: Japan International Cooperation Agency. 2015. *Metro Manila Urban Transportation Integration Study Update and Capacity Enhancement Project Study*. Makati.

Similarly, Figure 12, which breaks down private and public transport modes in Metro Manila and its environs, indicates that motorcycles and cars are almost equal in share, while tricycle accounts for slightly lower share than the jeepney. This observation illustrates the importance of motorcycles as either a private or public mode of transport even in Metro Manila.

Figure 13 shows the movements of people or goods between different locations (desire line) of various modes and indicates that motorcycle usage is not only used for shorter trips as it even approximates the desire lines for other modes. This is true for jeepney, bus, and, more remarkably, for car desire lines. Figure 13, therefore, highlights the information given in previous figures and tables.

Looking at the Metropolitan Manila Development Authority (MMDA) statistics on major thoroughfares in Metro Manila with respect to annual average daily traffic, Table 12 supports the desire lines of modes shown in Figure 13. This, again, confirms the findings related to the motorcycle becoming a significant mode of transport in Metro Manila. A JICA study (2019) also calibrated their traffic surveys to include motorcycles as major modes of transport for trips in Metro Manila, and the results are shown in Tables 13 and 14. The calibration was done because motorcycles are becoming a significant part of the daily trips in Metro Manila.

Figure 13: Desire Line Charts by Travel Mode

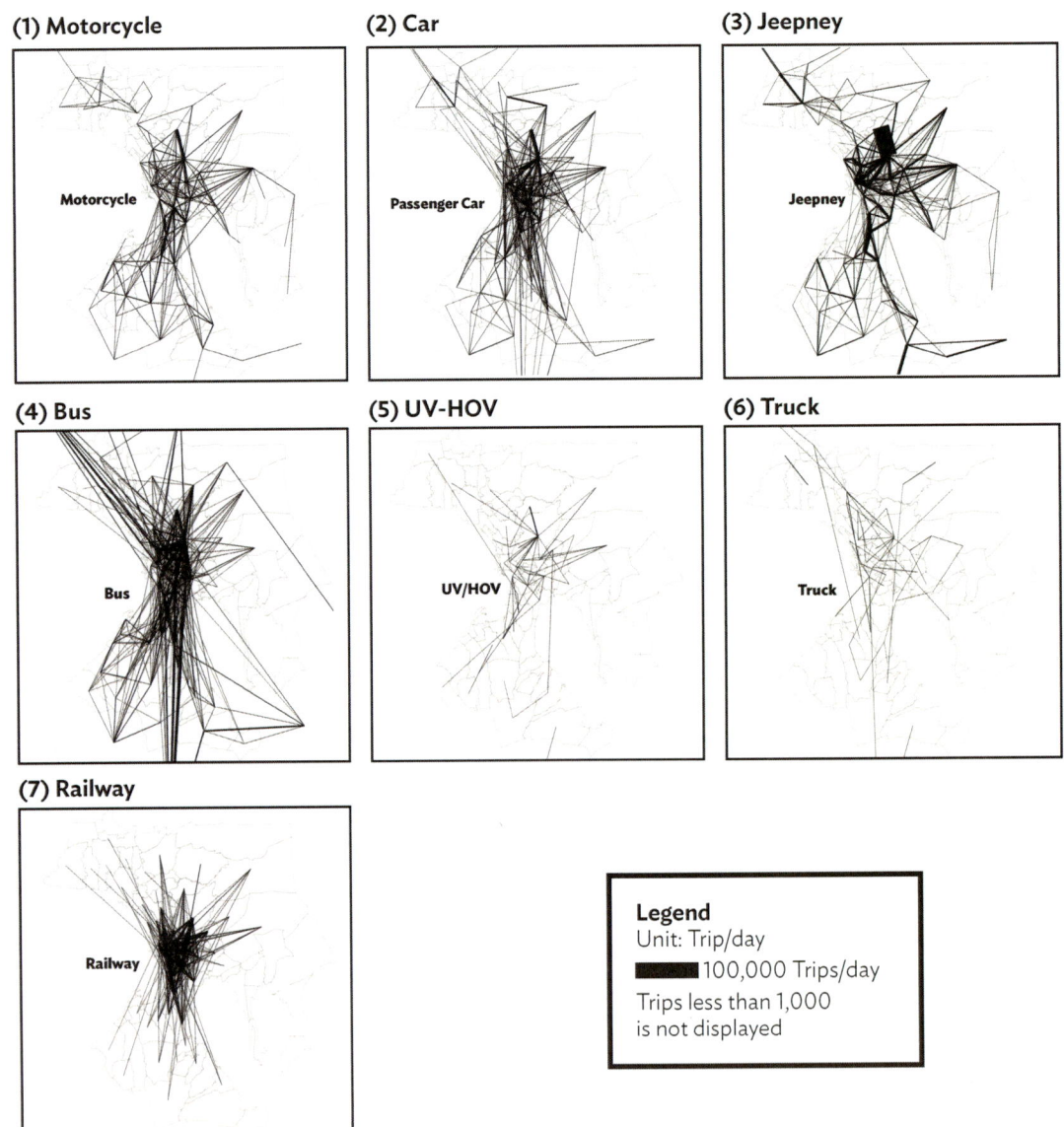

UV-HOV = utility vehicle-high-occupancy vehicle.

Source: Japan International Cooperation Agency. 2015. *Metro Manila Urban Transportation Integration Study Update and Capacity Enhancement Project Study.* Makati.

Table 12: Metropolitan Manila Development Authority Traffic Count Result, 2015

	Road Name	Metro Manila Annual Average Daily Traffic in 2015 ('000 vehicle/day)					
		Car	Jeepney	Bus	Truck	MC	Total
C:1	Recto	30	16	1	1	23	71
C:2	Mendoza	63	0	0	4	24	92
	Pres. Quirino	76	5	0	6	29	120
C:3	Araneta Ave.	55	2	0	4	28	90
C:4	EDSA (Buendia Ave.)	284	3	14	5	60	368
C:5	Katipunan/C.P. Garcia	135	1	1	10	46	194
R:1	Roxas Blvd.	138	0	0	1	34	173
R:2	Taft Ave.	56	16	3	1	15	91
R:3	SSH	87	0	1	7	28	127
R:4	Shaw Blvd.	59	10	0	2	25	95
R:5	Ortigas Ave.	73	10	1	5	32	121
R:6	Magsaysay Blvd.	57	13	1	2	26	100
	Aurora Blvd.	56	17	0	2	19	94
R:7	Quezon Ave.	136	8	1	4	35	186
	Commonwealth Ave.	169	17	6	6	60	259
R:8	A. Bonifacio	26	5	2	7	16	58
R:9	Rizal Ave.	29	13	0	2	26	70
R:10	Del Pan	0	0	0	0	0	0
Marcos Hwy.		112	17	0	6	37	173
MacArthur Hwy.		37	10	3	4	28	82
Total		**1,679**	**163**	**34**	**81**	**592**	**2,564**

MC = motorcycle, SSH = South Super Highway.
Source: Japan International Cooperation Agency. Philippines: Follow-up Survey on Roadmap for Transport Infrastructure Development for Greater Capital Region. Unpublished.

Table 13: Validation with Screen Line

	Motorcycle	Car	Jeepney	Bus	Truck	Total
Survey ('000 pax)	354	955	429	1,367	69	3,174
Forecast ('000 pax)	333	1,048	416	1,446	75	3,318
Forecast/Survey	0.94	1.10	0.97	1.06	1.09	1.05

Source: Japan International Cooperation Agency. Philippines: Follow-up Survey on Roadmap for Transport Infrastructure Development for Greater Capital Region. Unpublished.

Table 14: Validation with Cordon Line

		Motorcycle	Car	Jeepney	Bus	Truck	Total	Forecast/Survey
North Part	Survey ('000 pax)	157	87	196	65	20	526	1.10
	Forecast ('000 pax)	168	106	256	30	19	579	
East Part	Survey ('000 pax)	317	550	532	31	7	1,477	0.91
	Forecast ('000 pax)	207	524	512	56	45	1,344	
South Part	Survey ('000 pax)	118	174	210	85	16	603	1.05
	Forecast ('000 pax)	119	178	281	97	17	693	
Total	Survey ('000 pax)	593	811	938	181	83	2,606	1.04
	Forecast ('000 pax)	494	808	1,049	184	81	2,616	
	Forecast/Survey	0.83	1.00	1.12	1.02	0.98	1.00	

Source: Japan International Cooperation Agency. Philippines: Follow-up Survey on Roadmap for Transport Infrastructure Development for Greater Capital Region. Unpublished.

As modes of public transport, motorcycles come in the form of tricycle, *habal-habal, motorela,* and *bajaj,* among others. The last three are usually found in the provinces, but *habal-habal* has become popular in Metro Manila for the past 10 years. In fact, with the developments in information and communication technology, the *habal-habal* has evolved into a public transport system that is personalized and can be accessed through wireless mobile applications, such as GrabBike and Angkas. As such, the motorcycle-driven public transport is fast becoming a legitimate mode through a systematic and apps-based transport method, similar to neighboring Southeast Asian countries like Indonesia and Viet Nam. The Land Transportation Franchising Regulatory Board allowed a 6-month pilot run for Angkas in Metro Manila and Cebu City (in Cebu province) starting June 2019.

Aside from commuting, motorcycles are now becoming popular for delivery services. The application of information and communication technology in transport through mobile applications and the internet contributed to the development and promotion of such systems. Services such as Lalamove provide delivery services to businesses and individuals, carrying items such as documents, parcels, and other products. The popularity of such services are considered to have been due to the convenience enjoyed by its users. Food delivery services such as GrabFood and Foodpanda tend to compete against in-house delivery services. Payment can be done using mobile phone credits that can be converted to cash.

Informal interviews of random drivers of Angkas, an on-demand app-based motorcycle taxi service, revealed that they are not full-time or regular employees. Most have regular jobs and drive for Angkas during their free time, usually at night and on weekends. Driving for 3 to 4 hours a day for Angkas gives them the opportunity to supplement their existing income. Earnings range from ₱500 to ₱800 (equivalent to about $9 to $15) for a 3-hour shift, and higher if there is more demand or less traffic congestion. Riders have been known to be able to earn as much as ₱1,500 (about $28) in one shift.

GrabFood, on the other hand, does not provide similar incentives. Some drivers, who were interviewed informally, claim that the service requires them to queue, order, and pay first on behalf of the customer, making it time-consuming and sometimes costly for the drivers. Despite these challenges and risks, riders continue to seek out this source of income.

Given the rise of motorcycle usage for online delivery and its popularity among consumers, there is a need to look deeper into these services, particularly the behavior drivers and whether or not this correlates to the increase in motorcycle-related crashes. A significant number of drivers joining these services have regular jobs and may be susceptible to fatigue, for example.

Aside from road safety, there may also be a need to regulate companies and introduce industry standards to maintain or improve service levels. Infrastructure support in the form of enhanced information and communication systems, including road and other related facilities, may also be needed.

Another concern that needs to be addressed is the motorcycle drivers' tendency to converge in areas allotted for pedestrians, usually at pedestrian crossings and sidewalks near commercial establishments. There is a need to see if integrating facilities for this purpose in the planning of transport infrastructure, especially in commercial or mixed-use areas, is worth exploring.

A further concern that was raised on the proliferation of motorcycles as a mode for commuting is that it may result in drivers maneuvering recklessly and displaying behavior similar to drivers in the public transport sector, thus leading to road crashes.

Table 15 illustrates the trend of road crashes involving motorcycles, including tricycles. It can be concluded that the increase in the usage of motorcycles have contributed to the increase in road crashes in Metro Manila. It is imperative that strategies toward minimizing road crashes involving motorcycles should also be put in place. A framework is needed to address motorcycle usage and minimize road crashes.

General discussions on road crashes are given in the Appendix. The information employed in the discussions comes from MMDA, which collects and updates data annually.

Table 15: Vehicles Involved in Road Crashes in Metro Manila, 2010–2017

Vehicle	2010	2011	2012	2013	2014	2015	2016	2017
Motorcycle	17,666	17,837	19,574	20,272	20,515	20,283	23,105	24,058
Tricycle	3,221	3,463	3,669	3,824	3,595	3,666	3,773	3,655
Car	72,906	71,393	75,880	79,918	78,970	90,629	108,307	110,653
Jeepney	11,296	11,424	11,937	11,853	11,106	10,741	11,157	10,163
Taxi	7,927	7,343	11,067	13,868	12,511	9,652	8,360	6,378
Bus	7,633	6,940	6,752	6,435	6,266	7,371	9,563	9,214
Van	11,579	12,117	8,103	6,041	13,930	15,774	18,772	20,940
Truck	9,488	9,480	11,791	12,996	15,188	17,268	19,614	17,858
Total	**141,716**	**139,997**	**148,773**	**155,207**	**162,081**	**175,384**	**202,651**	**202,919**

Source: Government of the Philippines, Metropolitan Manila Development Authority. *Metro Manila Accident Reporting and Analysis System* (2010–2017).

The next section elaborates on an initial policy framework suggested given the findings presented in this study. It is also hoped that with the policy framework, the usage of motorcycles as a principal mode of transport for commuting and delivery will improve.

Policy and Responsive Initiatives to Address Motorcycle Usage in Metro Manila

An initial policy framework (Figure 14) is presented with the intention of addressing motorcycle-related crashes, particularly in Metro Manila. This framework is anchored mainly on "soft" and "hard" measures that are considered based on best practices and literature on motorcycle crashes. Motorcycle usage is incorporated in the framework to find strategies in addressing road crashes and improving the levels of services of motorcycles as a main mode of transport.

Figure 14: Motorcycle Road Safety Policy Framework

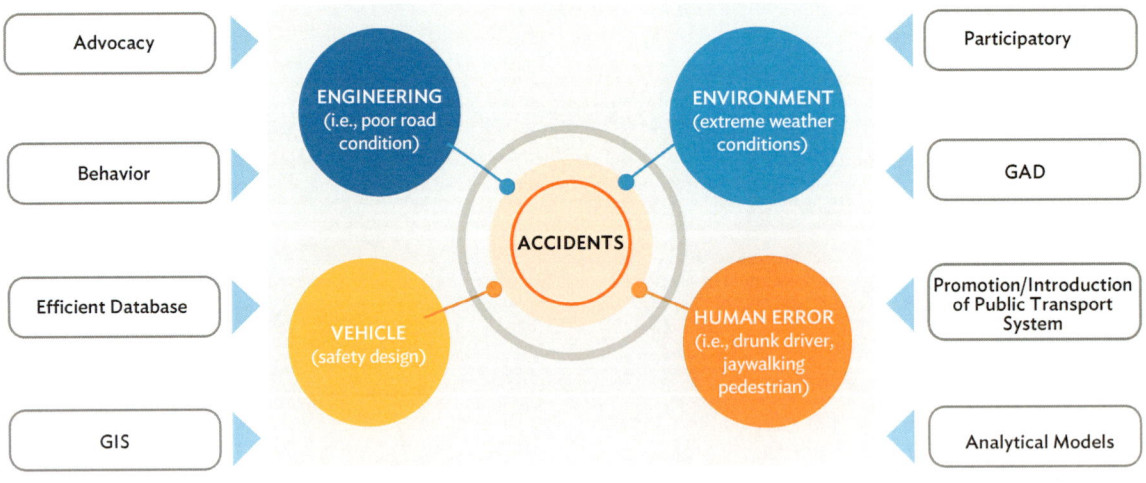

GAD = gender and development, GIS = geographic information system.
Note: This is a proposed framework based on findings from the study.
Source: ADB.

The overview of the motorcycle road safety policy framework is anchored on several factors. The impact of motorcycle usage, however, is not mentioned; the nearest element is the presence of behavior in the framework. The road safety policy framework must thus include usage of motorcycles. This is important since usage affects both the behavior of the motorcycle drivers and passengers, and the goods being transported. Goods are taken into consideration since these not only include documents, packages, or parcels, but also food, which need special handling and care. The lack of proper food containers, for example, can affect driving behavior and may cause road crashes.

It is also worth mentioning that proper training and education of motorcycle drivers should be an industry requirement. Though Angkas and Grab have their own training, it may be worth professionalizing these and provide proper guidance and accreditation; the Technical Education and Skills Development Authority can be the proper institution, in this regard. A new training program providing not only driving and road safety education, but also proper conduct and behavior and social manners needs to be incorporated. The issuance of driver certification and accreditation can also be anchored on this program to help ensure professionalism and awareness on safe driving and road courtesy.

Local planning and development of road infrastructure also needs consider to road safety for motorcycles. Designing facilities such as terminals, either for public transport or delivery service, can help minimize the presence of motorcycles on major roads and thoroughfares.

On roads, proper lane markings for motorcycles can help ensure appropriate segregation of vehicles.

Safety measures being advocated by the MMDA should be incorporated in coming up with policies for motorcycle usage as public transport and delivery service. Pertinent laws such as the Public Service Act should be reviewed and, if necessary, amended. This will ensure that motorcycle usage, in the context of public transport and logistics, is recognized.

Conclusions

The study attempted to understand the increased usage of motorcycles. Though the study focuses on Metro Manila in the Philippines, the there is a similar growth trend in other countries in Southeast Asia.

Recent developments in information and communication technology, particularly the use of internet and mobile applications, contributed to the increase in motorcycle usage.

Desire lines of various travel modes indicated that motorcycles now approximate that of cars and other public transport modes. Motorcycles have become part of daily commuting and integral in logistics services. This study presented and discussed issues related to this, and put forward suggestions on addressing these issues.

A road safety policy framework is presented and motorcycle usage in the context of user behavior is introduced. Capacity building and strategies to enhance road safety are proposed. It is also suggested that motorcycles be considered among primary modes for commuting and logistics, and that the Public Service Act be reviewed and amended as appropriate. Planning and design of facilities, notably at the local level, should consider motorcycle usage and its requirements.

Through this study, it is hoped that awareness on motorcycle usage, in terms of road safety and transport planning, will be part of the government policy making and gather support from different sectors.

Appendix: Statistical Data on Road Crashes in Metro Manila

Data from figures and tables in this section indicate that transport and traffic problems are complex because actual causes are interrelated and require a comprehensive approach. Traffic congestion is always the main issue and less focus is given to road safety. The Government of the Philippines, through the Metropolitan Manila Development Authority (MMDA), has, to a certain degree, focused attention on road safety, given the high economic costs of road accidents. Insurance companies are already regularly studying the impacts on their industry.

Discussions in this study present statistics and findings of the MMDA, through its Metro Manila Accident Reporting and Analysis System (MMARAS), which has its beginnings in 2005 under the Road Safety Unit of MMDA Traffic Discipline Office-Traffic Engineering Center. The MMDA is cooperating with various traffic investigation units of the Philippine National Police in Metro Manila. MMARAS aims to monitor road crashes and mitigate its occurrences.

Based on the MMARAS report, the actual number of fatalities in 2017 was 434 persons per 423 recorded cases of road crash, compared to 446 persons per 426 recorded cases in 2016. This may imply that engineering solutions and interventions by the MMDA toward road safety has become more effective. In 2017, there were 19,374 persons injured in Metro Manila's roads, a decrease of 7.19% from 20,876 persons injured in 2016 (Table A1).

Although the reported road crashes displayed an increasing trend from 2011 to 2017 (Figure A1), it is worth mentioning that the trend is not as sharp compared to previous years, thus supporting the information provided in Table A1.

Figure A1: Road Crash Statistical Trends

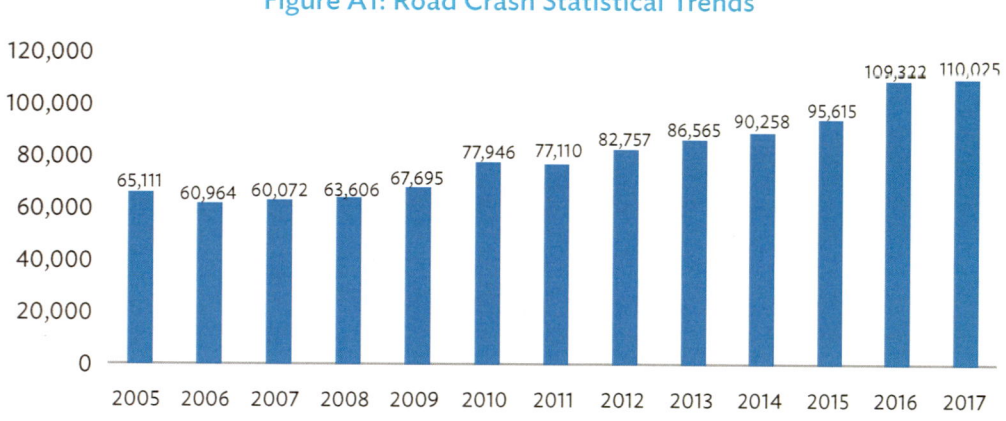

Source: Government of the Philippines, Metropolitan Manila Development Authority. 2017. *Metro Manila Accident Reporting and Analysis System*. Makati.

Table A1: Comparison of Statistics, 2016 and 2017

Year	Total Number of Fatalities	Total Number of Injuries
2016	446	20,876
2017	434	19,374

Source: Government of the Philippines, Metropolitan Manila Development Authority. 2017. *Metro Manila Accident Reporting and Analysis System*. Makati.

Table A2 categorizes road crashes in Metro Manila based on property damage and injury. Quezon City registered the highest number of road crashes.

Table A2: Road Crashes by District or City

District/City	Damage to Property	Fatal	Non-Fatal Injury	Total
Central (Quezon)	30,633	132	4,729	35,494
Eastern (Mandaluyong)	4,925	7	553	5,485
Eastern (Marikina)	3,446	14	1,158	4,618
Eastern (Pasig)	6,721	23	681	7,425
Eastern (Pateros)	2	1	1	4
Eastern (San Juan)	1,582	2	225	1,809
Northern (Caloocan)	3,288	31	851	4,170
Northern (Malabon)	784	13	421	1,218
Northern (Navotas)	641	6	381	1,028
Northern (Valenzuela)	1,025	29	745	1,799
Southern (Las Piñas)	2,691	11	653	3,355
Southern (Makati)	10,680	18	727	11,425
Southern (Muntinlupa)	3,316	13	800	4,129
Southern (Parañaque)	4,149	41	992	5,182
Southern (Pasay)	5,099	14	699	5,812
Southern (Taguig)	5,116	15	626	5,757
Western (Manila)	9,999	53	1,263	11,315
Total	**94,097**	**423**	**15,505**	**110,025**

Source: Government of the Philippines, Metropolitan Manila Development Authority. 2017. *Metro Manila Accident Reporting and Analysis System*. Makati.

The MMARAS Annual Report 2017 report cites the following factors why Quezon City recorded the highest number of road crashes:

- central business districts and high social and economic activity;
- bigger land area than other cities in Metro Manila; and
- the presence of major road networks such as Epifanio de los Santos Avenue, C-5 Road, and Commonwealth Avenue.

The MMARAS report classifies persons involved in road crashes by age (Table A3). Those involved in road crashes typically range from 17 to 65 years old, with the highest number belonging to the 18 to 51 years old age group. This suggests that persons from these age brackets are more mobile.

Table A3: Road Crashes by Age

Age Bracket	Fatal	Non-Fatal Injury	Total
01-17	4	136	140
18-34	163	6,182	6,345
35-51	91	3,589	3,680
52-65	37	1,115	1,152
66- above	22	356	378
Total	**317**	**11,378**	**11,695**

Source: Government of the Philippines, Metropolitan Manila Development Authority. 2017. *Metro Manila Accident Reporting and Analysis System*. Makati.

Table A4, meanwhile, shows the number of vehicles involved in road crashes. As expected, cars had the highest number, followed by motorcycles. The number of road crashes increased slightly from 2016 to 2017—by 2.2% to 2,346 for cars and by 4.1% to 953 for motorcycles. The increase in road crashes associated with motorcycles tends to support the correlation with the increased usage of motorcycles for various purposes. This may need a deeper look to come up with more mitigation measures.

Table A4: Number of Vehicles and Casualties in Road Crashes, 2017

Type of Vehicle	Number of Vehicles	Actual Number of Casualties Involved in Road Crash					
		Driver Deaths	Driver Injuries	Passenger Deaths	Passenger Injuries	Pedestrian Deaths	Pedestrian Injuries
Bike/Pedicab	1,431	21	807	1	116	2	50
Motorcycle	24,058	178	7,905	37	2,292	32	1,985
Tricycle	3,655	11	611	3	755	3	243
Car	110,653	46	4,227	15	2,209	36	1,245
PUJ	10,163	9	682	11	1,152	13	428
Taxi	6,378	5	428	2	309	5	136
Bus	9,214	7	273	5	461	10	140
Van	20,940	17	936	4	609	13	303
Truck	17,858	58	745	13	646	47	244
Train	18	-	1	-	5	9	4
Unknown	5,668	8	214	1	122	9	198

PUJ = public utility jeepney.
Source: Government of the Philippines, Metropolitan Manila Development Authority. 2017. *Metro Manila Accident Reporting and Analysis System*. Makati.

The following tables from the MMARAS report show statistics on road crashes in major corridors in Metro Manila.

Table A5: Road Crashes along EDSA City Routes

District/(City)	Damage to Property	Fatal	Non-Fatal Injury	Total
Central (Quezon)	5,651	8	379	6,038
Eastern (Mandaluyong)	2,076	1	114	2,191
Eastern (San Juan)	131	1	8	140
Northern (Caloocan)	415	3	37	455
Southern (Makati)	2,464	4	121	2,589
Southern (Pasay)	1,103	2	117	1,222
Total	**11,840**	**19**	**776**	**12,635**

Source: Government of the Philippines, Metropolitan Manila Development Authority. 2017. *Metro Manila Accident Reporting and Analysis System*. Makati.

Table A6: Road Crashes along EDSA Accident-Prone Areas

Location	Fatal	Non-Fatal Injury	Total
Harrison Street–Roxas Boulevard		32	32
Kamuning–NIA Road		63	63
North Avenue–Corregidor Street	3	48	51
Rochester–Ortigas–Guadix		34	34
Shaw Boulevard–SM Megamall	1	41	42
Total	**4**	**218**	**222**

Source: Government of the Philippines, Metropolitan Manila Development Authority. 2017. *Metro Manila Accident Reporting and Analysis System*. Makati.

Table A7: Road Crashes along C5 Road

Month	Damage to Property	Fatal	Non-Fatal Injury	Total
January	529		61	590
February	506	2	42	550
March	523	3	60	586
April	364	3	46	413
May	425	2	58	485
June	559		59	618
July	477	2	45	524
August	407	2	42	451
September	367	2	37	406
October	412	4	45	461
November	313	2	39	354
December	311	1	44	356
Total	**5,193**	**23**	**578**	**5,794**

Source: Government of the Philippines, Metropolitan Manila Development Authority. 2017. *Metro Manila Accident Reporting and Analysis System*. Makati.

Table A8: Road Crashes along C5 Accident-Prone Areas

Location	Fatal	Non-Fatal Injury	Total
C. P. Garcia Avenue–Pansol Magsaysay Avenue	1	39	40
Bagong Ilog Flyover–Caltex Gas Station	2	37	39
Libis Interchange–Blue Ridge Area	2	29	31
Market Market–SM Aura	1	28	29
SM Warehouse	2	26	28
Total	**8**	**159**	**167**

Source: Government of the Philippines, Metropolitan Manila Development Authority. 2017. *Metro Manila Accident Reporting and Analysis System*. Makati.

Table A9: Monthly Road Crashes along C5 Road

Month	Damage to Property	Fatal	Non-Fatal Injury	Total
January	353		84	437
February	327		65	392
March	305	1	57	363
April	256	2	46	304
May	300	2	69	371
June	381	4	80	465
July	438	1	78	517
August	248	1	57	306
September	327		59	386
October	328	3	58	389
November	321		43	364
December	308	3	44	355
Total	**3,892**	**17**	**740**	**4,649**

Source: Government of the Philippines, Metropolitan Manila Development Authority. 2017. *Metro Manila Accident Reporting and Analysis System*. Makati.

Table A10: Road Crashes along Commonwealth Avenue Accident-Prone Areas

Location	Fatal	Non-Fatal Injury	Total
COA–Riverside Street	2	27	29
IBP Road (Sandigan) –Meralco–BF Road	1	40	41
Luzon Avenue–Puregold	2	23	25
Tandang Sora Avenue	2	78	80
Techno Hub–AIT Building		28	28
Total	**7**	**221**	**228**

Source: Government of the Philippines, Metropolitan Manila Development Authority. 2017. *Metro Manila Accident Reporting and Analysis System*. Makati.

These updates suggest that with continuous efforts and cooperation, road crashes can be minimized, thus suggestions or recommendations in the study are worth considering.

References

Japan International Cooperation Agency. 2015. *Metro Manila Urban Transportation Integration Study Update and Capacity Enhancement Project Study*. Makati.

——. Philippines: Follow-up Survey on Roadmap for Transport Infrastructure Development for Greater Capital Region. Unpublished.

Government of the Philippines, Metropolitan Manila Development Authority. 2010. *Metro Manila Accident Reporting and Analysis System*. Makati.

——. 2011. *Metro Manila Accident Reporting and Analysis System*. Makati.

——. 2012. *Metro Manila Accident Reporting and Analysis System*. Makati.

——. 2013. *Metro Manila Accident Reporting and Analysis System*. Makati.

——. 2014. *Metro Manila Accident Reporting and Analysis System*. Makati.

——. 2015. *Metro Manila Accident Reporting and Analysis System*. Makati.

——. 2016. *Metro Manila Accident Reporting and Analysis System*. Makati.

——. 2017. *Metro Manila* Accident Reporting and Analysis System. Makati.

Government of the Philippines, Philippine Statistics Authority. 2017. *2017 Philippine Statistical Yearbook*. Quezon City.

——. 2018. *2018 Philippine Statistical Yearbook*. Quezon City.

World Health Organization. 2015. *Global Status Report on Road Safety*. Geneva.

——. 2018. *Global Status Report on Road Safety*. Geneva.

Lightning Source UK Ltd.
Milton Keynes UK
UKRC020027080820
367832UK00006B/24